Lo siento / Saying I'm Sorry

Kathleen Connors
Traducido por Nathalie Beullens-Maoui

Gareth Stevens
PUBLISHING

conceptos básicos

¿Le has quitado alguna vez un juguete a tu hermana?

Have you ever taken a toy from your sister?

A lo mejor le dijiste algo desagradable a un compañero de clase.

Maybe you said mean things to a boy in your class.

No siempre podemos ser agradables todo el tiempo.

No one is nice all the time.

Pero puedes tratar de hacer las paces por lo que hiciste.

But you can try to make up for what you have done.

Si heriste o lastimaste
a alguien, dile que
lo sientes.

If you have hurt or
bothered someone,
you can say
you are sorry.

Piensa en cómo se debe sentir la persona que lastimaste.

Think about how the person you hurt must feel.

Si dices "lo siento" eso indica que te arrepientes de lo que hiciste.

Saying "I'm sorry" means you feel bad for what you did.

Cuando dices "lo siento", le comunicas a la otra persona que entiendes porqué se siente dolida.

Saying "I'm sorry" lets others know you understand why they are hurt.

A veces con solo decir "lo siento" es suficiente.

Saying "I'm sorry" is sometimes enough.

Pero otras veces a lo mejor prefieres *demostrarle* que de verdad lo sientes.

Other times, you might want to *show* that you are sorry.

N8143S

Un abrazo o compartir
un juguete es una buena
forma de demostrarlo.

Giving a hug
or sharing a toy
is a good way
to do that!

Please visit our website, www.garethstevens.com. For a free color catalog of all our high-quality books, call toll free 1-800-542-2595 or fax 1-877-542-2596.

Library of Congress Cataloging-in-Publication Data

Connors, Kathleen.
Saying I'm sorry = Lo siento / Kathleen Connors.
p. cm. — (Minding Our Manners = Cuida tus modales)
Parallel title: Cuida tus modales.
In English and Spanish.
Includes index.
ISBN 978-1-4824-1739-5 (library binding)
1. Apologizing—Juvenile literature. 2. Children—Conduct of life. I. Title. II. Title: Saying I am sorry.
BF575.A75C66 2015
395—dc23

First Edition

Published in 2015 by
Gareth Stevens Publishing
111 East 14th Street, Suite 349
New York, NY 10003

Designer: Andrea Davison-Bartolotta
Editor: Kristen Rajczak
Spanish Translation: Nathalie Beullens-Maoui

Photo credits: Cover, p. 1 David Laurens/PhotoAlto Agency RF Collections/Getty Images; p. 3 Colin Hawkins/Cultura/Getty Images; p. 5 Monkey Business Images Ltd/Monkey Business/Thinkstock; p. 7 Robert Niedring/Getty Images; p. 9 Alexey Shinkevich/Shutterstock.com; p. 11 Olimpik/Shutterstock.com; p. 13 Voyagerix/iStock/Thinkstock; p. 15 Mel Yates/The Image Bank/Getty Images; p. 17 Image Source/Getty Images; p. 19 Pressmaster/Shutterstock.com; p. 21 Randy Faris/Fuse/Thinkstock; p. 23 Nicole S. Young/iStock/Thinkstock.

Printed in the United States of America

CPSIA compliance information: Batch #CW15GS: For further information contact Gareth Stevens, New York, New York at 1-800-542-2595.